Dec 2021
with gratitude
Maggie

CW00731111

MOUNTAIN NOTES

A Nature Diary by Maggie Doyle

Copyright © Maggie Doyle 2021

Published by Magysfarm.co.uk 2021

ISBN 978 1 914408 66 3

A CIP catalogue record for this book in available from the British library

Extract from 'Changes' by Seamus Heaney used with kind permission of Faber and Faber Ltd

All photographs taken by Maggie with thanks to Ken at lucascreativeart.co.uk for additional artwork.

Cover design by Elsa Schade-Weskott

Printed and bound in Great Britain by
Biddles Books Limited, King's Lynn, Norfolk

Dedication

In Loving memory of my parents Nicholas and Margaret Doyle

Dedicated to my sister Carmel, my husband Linley and godson Jamie

"*This is a beautiful, important book that tells the story of a time, a love and a place that changed a life. Its themes of belonging, community and nature sing off the page; exploring what it means to live respectfully and meaningfully; something so many of us are drawn to more than ever before. Maggie's story will touch your heart and lead you by the hand; back to the gorgeous world outside your door.*"

Kerri Ni Dochartaigh

"*A beautiful and lilting meditation on returning home to an ancestral farm in Northern Ireland. This wild chorale is filled with cairns and mountains, heather and hedgerows, and a special starling. A memorable and musical book of nature and place.*"

Kathryn Aalto

Contents

'So tender, I said, 'Remember this.
It will be good for you to retrace this path
when you have grown away and stand at last
at the very centre of the empty city.'

from 'Changes' by Seamus Heaney

Prologue

The wild music of Spring mornings is my favourite sound of home. Up here in the rugged Dromara Hills, the chorus rises with the sun as it floats up over Slieve Croob, Slievenaboley, Slievegarran, Slievenisky, Cratlieve and Dechomet. All the peaks awakening as the first shafts of light pierce the darkness.

The songbirds start early to tell their stories in tiny notes that sparkle in the sleeping trees. Robins and wrens, blackbirds and starlings, all piping softly in the pre-dawn, increasing their volume as the light gets stronger. They were singing the morning my father Nicholas died on the 4th of May 1974. I like to believe that the sweetness of their songs eased his passing from this world to the next.

I grew up on this farm at the foot of Dechomet Mountain in the Dromara Hills, Northern Ireland. It was a small dairy farm where my mother milked eight cows twice every day for years after Daddy died, following a short illness from cancer. I was twelve years old, my sister Carmel was eight and for the three of us the loss was immeasurable. But life on the farm had to go on and, together, we took good care of our cows because they were our breadwinners and our friends. Every morning, three steel cans of cooled milk were rolled from the dairy to the roadside for the Creamery lorry to pick up. Each Friesian cow had a name and sometimes, in the summer, my mother Maggie would wander down into the fields to talk to them – Whitey, Wee heifer, Margaret Hill, Toddles and the rest. They would walk up to her and push their big heads under her arm for a cuddle. Cows are kind that way and the bond between us and the animals was strong and unforgettable. In 1990, my mother had to retire from farming and all the cows were sold. The farmyard was silent for years while I was working in Belfast city but, in my heart, I always knew I would go back to the fields and the homeplace.

In 2018 my husband Linley and I were planning to leave the city to go back to the farm. We wanted to build a new home and a music venue there. One bright Spring morning, I drove up to the hills to say goodbye to the old house and give thanks for the shelter we once knew there. As I turned the key in the lock, I noticed the faded, red velvet curtains in the living room were disturbed and pushed apart. With an anxious heart, I crept into the empty room to find twigs, some strands of wool and barley straws lying in the scattered ashes on the carpet in front of the old hearth. As I knelt down to have a closer look, there was a sudden, fluttering clatter in the hallway followed by an uneasy silence.

I waited fearfully, watching the open door that led to the hall. Within minutes she stepped lightly into the room, twisting her head from side to side and pecking at the carpet. A dainty, yellow-beaked starling – her iridescent plumage shimmering in the morning sun. When our eyes met, the room froze like a stopped clock. I knelt transfixed on the floor, the starling watching me with dark, unblinking eyes.

'What took you so long?' she asked, shaking the soot off her purpled feathers.

'I didn't know you were here,' I said, humbled. 'But you can't build here – it's not safe. This house is coming down.'

'Then you have to set me free! I have more work to do out there,' she said, flying up on to the windowsill and scratching furiously at the glass.

Very slowly, with my heart racing, I crept up behind her and gently grasped the little velvet body in my cupped hands. In the sunlit silence, I carried her like a flickering candle to the back door and set her free.

'I'm sorry,' I said. 'Will you come back someday... please?'

'Look for me in the spring trees,' she cried, her silhouette disappearing into the high sycamores. I said goodbye to the old house and drove away.

In January 2020 we were happily settled in our new home and busy making plans to run a small music club in a restored barn where the cows used to feed their calves. In this ancient place where my grandfather had also kept his heavy horses and ploughs, we created a performance space with room for a small audience. We were preparing new ground where music could flourish on the farm. One fine Spring morning, as the sun rose over the hills, I stood listening to the wild chorale of dawn birds. In the choir, I thought I could hear her. A tiny voice lilting up in the sycamores, announcing the homecoming.

Winter sun over Mourne
from Slieve Croob

January

It's the 1st of January 2020 and the world is at my feet. From the summit of Slieve Croob, I can see the past draining down the funnel of the old year, leaving a weak but hopeful sun hiding in the washed-out light of the winter sky. Every New Year's Day, I stand at the crest of this mountain in the Dromara Hills and stare back at the old year. I've been doing this for decades, just being at peace with the mountain, letting go of the past with gratitude in order to move on. It's the place I return to time after time, to touch the sky and reset my heart.

Slieve Croob means 'mountain of the hoof' and the sheep own the slopes here, grazing quietly in the foothills of the high Mournes. The path from the small carpark is inviting as it winds skywards through bog cotton, heather and sedge. The gurgling baby Lagan spills downwards through the marsh grass, laughing at the wind and gathering strength for the charge to the widening riverbed below. It's always reassuring to stand here at the source – a baptism of sorts, cleansing and renewing. This is the land of stiles and streams, little gateways to new beginnings and it has been calling me home from Belfast city for years. The walk forces me to breathe more deeply, to focus on the road ahead and reach for the sky. In the distance, I see the golden cranes of Harland and Wolff flash in the city estuary, where the river finishes its race. In my heart, I know it wants to turn back too, rushing upwards to the little townlands of Dree and Drinn, Finnis and Begney, where the landscape is softer and the light is rainbowed.

I feel so small standing here on the path that narrows to present a crown of cairns spread out across the summit – Neolithic burial chambers holding centuries of secrets, resting in peace here on this wild mountainscape. Twelve kings are said to buried here, nameless monarchs who took with them to the grave their tales of battles won and lost. The ancient views are spectacular and humbling, and on the south face I see the ghosts of chieftains bow in awe at the panorama of peaks gleaming in the distant Mourne kingdom. Backlit by the white-gold light of the hidden sun, Slieve

Donard is every inch the leader after whom it was named – strong, dependable and always there for me and the gazing world. For this, I am so grateful, and whisper a silent prayer of thanks for the chance to come back to this landscape that is so dear to me.

ﷺ

January skies are layered in shades of slate and stone, and on the 14th day, the mountain sheep are spreading out, taking shelter from the threatening wind behind clumps of weathered rushes and whin bushes. From my kitchen window, I watch the relentless rain beating down on the slender fir trees at the bottom of the garden. A weather bomb in the form of Storm Brendan has exploded on our horizon. Eighty-miles-an-hour winds from deep out in the Atlantic are shaking our world, and it is shocking to witness. The lights are blinking and I am afraid of the early darkness that will creep soon down over Dechomet Mountain.

I wait in silence for this storm to pass. The clock's tick-tock is comforting as I try not to think about the forecast predicting Brendan to be the first storm of many this year. Among the firs, I focus on the dead tree still standing in the storm, a ghost among the greenery. Translucent and skeletal, it stands tall in its nakedness, refusing to bend. Such dignity and inner strength. Not ready to go. 'We'll just lie low beneath the whins,' I tell you, Linley. And so we do, for days, until the world stops shaking.

In the farmyard, our little music barn waits for the first chords to push through, like green shoots from the old stones. Deep down below the floor it holds the memory of my dancing ancestors, spinning reels and jigs here at harvest time. The echo of their songs and laughter warms the empty space until the tilly lamp is relit when we welcome our music-making friends to the stage. In this cosy, whitewashed room with wooden floors and soft lighting, a first-class band of jazz musicians from the four corners of these islands is lead by Cork man Paul Dunlea in a swinging, elegiac suite about terrible beauties of the past. The trombone, saxophone and trumpet sounds soar in a wild chorus that echoes across the snowfields all around us. Outside, the mountain is pulsing with the adrenalin rush, and we all feel inspired on this new ground. Our hearts are reset; we are in time with ourselves.

Reflections on Ringsend Road

February

It's five o'clock in February and the world seems upside down. It's the 9th day, and I am walking through the archway of a double rainbow sitting high across the Ringsend Road. The air is thin and cold after an Arctic shower; I am shivery as I hurry home. At the foot of White's Hill, I am stopped by the sight of the sky drowning in the huge pools of rainwater on the roadside. The entire horizon is telescoped and perfectly mirrored in the floods, and I feel myself falling into the blue, sinking deeply beneath the clouds and rainbow into the Earth's core. Storm Ciara has caused widespread wind and flood damage across the country and brought a new perspective with a warning. Tread carefully when you walk on water, and take nothing for granted when the sky is beneath your feet.

I walk on, shaken and unsettled. There are little bursts of snowdrops trembling along the grass verges – tiny white fairy bells on a frozen ditch.

They have survived and are ringing joyously. I'm so glad to see them and to hear their music in the hedgerow.

The 13th brings another sleepless night with Storm Dennis thundering across the hills and trailing clouds of discord across the valley. An intense, extratropical cyclone, he has brought the full force of his rage to this high, exposed area, ripping slates and drainpipes off the shed in the farmyard. The roar and the speed of his arrival is almost biblical, and we are troubled as we watch the trees in our garden take another whipping.

I have booked a birdwatching tour with the local red kite group, as I'm keen to learn more about the graceful birds

I see hovering above the mountain most mornings. But standing here watching the Mournes drift in and out of the cloudscape, I am scared and reluctant to leave the house. You look at me and point to the mountain slope where a flock of blackface sheep are standing resolutely close to the whins with their backs to the storm. I nod and drive off, smiling in the gale, to the meeting point a few miles away.

We gather at a viewing site on the Bannonstown Road, which follows the tree line around the back of Castlewellan Forest Park. From across the valley it offers dramatic pictures of the Dromara Hills, Slieve Croob, Slievenisky, Slievenaboley, Slievegarran, Cratlieve and Dechomet. Slieve comes from the Irish word 'sliabh', meaning mountain. The landscape here is measurable only in geological time, formed over 400 million years ago, during several ice ages. Sheets of ice from Scotland and Donegal forced their way across the plains, carving out valleys and forming the Mourne Mountains range and these Dromara Hills. It's hard to fathom, really, because this place is in deep time. The ancient echoes are real to me and from somewhere in the belowland beneath the valley floor I hear the frozen notes of the ice sheet's song – dark, rich and sombre like a bowed double bass.

Shelagh, our red kite tour guide, welcomes our small group to her world of fabulous, graceful birds, which have been reintroduced to this area. She tells us the breeding pairs are thriving amongst the sycamores on the hills in the distance, and that we'll see them up close at the next observation point. She says they are the least threatening of the preying species, eating mostly small animals, already dead, found on roadsides and mountain ditches.

We drive on to the Lighthouse Road near Leitrim and huddle behind stone walls to watch for any activity. Shelagh tells us the kites love the thrill of a windy day, and soon she's pointing at the skies over Dechomet Mountain – named by Vikings in search of a good view of advancing enemies. With borrowed binoculars, I scan the familiar horizon; I feel a lump in my throat as I catch a glimpse of the red-breasted birds with golden-forked tails. They are sweeping and circling, singing to each other with high, distinctive mews.

They have no fear of the storm, strong and secure in their high-pitched songs. Enchanted by their grace, watching them dive and soar, I feel recharged and fully alive. The whole sky seems to belong to them and I just know these moments with the kites will enrich our days as this year unfolds.

As I drive home, the February sky is dimming, but in the half-light, I see the ghost of a rainbow. Shimmering strands of multi-coloured light reaching skywards above the dusk clouds to form the bow. Just on the edge of dark, the arch frames the mountain and then disappears, somewhere over the horizon, into a pool of violet and indigo.

Inside the music barn this evening, our friend Dana from Carolina is singing soulful songs infused with jazz and gospel music. She too has settled here in these hills with her family and she tells the story of her journey in her beautiful song 'Home Found Me'. Our small audience love the sentiment and, as her mellow tones melt out across the farmyard, I know that she too has placed her soul up here, over the rainbow, on the mountainscape with the kites.

The Fairy Thorn

March

It's early March and the world is frozen in silent frost-light. The news from the East is not good, and we have been warned to prepare for the change that Storm Corona will bring. The director general of the World Health Organization has declared that Covid-19, an illness caused by a new coronavirus, is now a pandemic, with thousands of people dying every day all over the world. He insists that urgent action must be taken to stop the spread of the disease. The world's alarm bell has been rung loud and clear.

In the mountains, snow has fallen overnight, and high upon the slopes it traces the ribbed remains of the lazy beds - a nineteenth-century reminder of hard times during the Irish Famine still printed on the landscape like a prayer. These patient hills have waited in a threatening darkness before. On the first weekend of the month, we drive around the back roads of the frozen landscape with two American friends Jim Beard and Jon Herington. They are outstanding musicians on tour in Ireland to promote their new album. We are all trying to be upbeat as I take them on a tour of local beauty spots. The road to the Windy Gap rises dramatically over the crest of Slievenaboley mountain to offer priceless views of the distant Mournes beyond the green valley below. We all stand in the wind where the buzzards soar and lose ourselves and our fears for a while in the landscape. At Legananny Dolmen, a five-thousand-year-old tripod of heavy stones, we take photographs with fixed smiles beneath the capstone of this Neolithic tomb. As our guests hurry back to the car, I wait for a while with Áine, the goddess for whom the dolmen was built in pre-Christian times. I am standing here looking for light in the remnants of the past. There is comfort in the strength of these ancient stones. I know they will survive the storm.

Back at the farm, I point to the little crowd of daffodils in a stone circle around the big sycamore at the bottom of our garden.

'Spring is here!' I tell our visitors, Jim and John, as the daffodils nod their heads in the breeze. They smile but I can see the faraway fear in their eyes as we check the evening news. Later, in the barn, our audience is spellbound as they deliver melodic twists and turns on piano and guitar that bounce off the whitewashed walls. The atmosphere is warm and intimate and we all want to stay in there in our bubble, but within days, their president is calling all Americans home. The world is shutting down to protect all of us from the coronavirus threat. In New York, the Broadway theatre district has gone dark and so too has our music barn.

え‍を

Up here, the light is changing now. The days are longer but not brighter, and you and I are locked down on the mountain.

Fastened in between the heather and hedgerows, we are pilgrims walking these country roads in search of comfort in the spring landscapes. On Drumgooland Road, we walk and talk of our fears for our families and our kind, elderly neighbours. We are still scared but hopeful that this storm will pass soon. On a grey, bleak afternoon, you stop suddenly to pick up a feather. It is a long, elegant feather, perfectly intact, as if dipped in bronze. I recognise the colours and my heart misses a beat. We walk a little further and find the limp, red body of a dead adult kite lying on the ditch with its beautiful head tucked under a damaged wing. Neither of us can speak. You place the single feather on the golden tail fork and we trudge home in silence.

In the evening, I'm watching the news reports from Italy where thousands of people are singing to each other from their balconies across the ancient squares. Their heads are up, defying the storm. My heart is breaking, and the tears flow uncontrollably. Out on the mountain, the kites are crying to each other across the treetops. They are feeling the loss too. An injury to one of us is an injury to us all.

These days are wide as they are long and I need to walk constantly on home ground. I'm taking you to the south side of Dechomet Mountain to see the Fairy Tree. It's a gnarly hawthorn that has grown sideways defiantly, like antlers pushing out of the stony slopes. I can see it from miles away, bolted on like a latch on the mountainside. It has survived perhaps a century of wild weather. 'It never lets go,' I tell you, as we get closer. Beneath the tree, many townlands are scattered across the drumlins below. Ballymacilreiny, Derryneil, Magheramayo Moneyslane and Gargory – little kingdoms, all sitting tight in the valley. The view is captivating and I blink as if waking to see a small, horned ewe appear from behind the rocks and run towards us before retreating to the tree. We step back and she lunges again. She is young and agile, with delicate black legs, and she wants us to go. We stumble away through the rocks and heather, breathless and bemused. I look back and see her standing, head held high, like a goddess guarding the tree with the Mourne panorama spread out behind her.

'I'm going to call her Yoelene,' I tell you, on the way back down the mountain.

'It suits her,' you reply.

On the 26th evening we are standing under a cold, crescent moon, hung low beneath Venus. We are in the garden to applaud, like millions of others, our friends and neighbours working in the National Health Service. It's dark, and I am sad for those lost and lonely in this storm. We start to clap slowly and the sound bounces off the mountain, splitting the darkness. I see our neighbours across the fields coming out of their front doors to do the same – the light spilling from hallways on to frozen ground. Within seconds, the valley is echoing with the sound of human hands uniting. The feeling of connection is deep and powerful. You bring out your trumpet and the heavy dusk lights up with the bright, golden notes of 'When the Saints Go Marching In' and suddenly, for just a little while, everyone is clapping in time across the valley. We are singing loudly and wildly, because every one of us wants to be in that number.

I am high on the joy of the moment and have an unexpected vision of a green amphitheatre in the valley, with an orchestra in full flow in the frost-light. There's a golden cloud above where second-realm voices sing out across the evening sky like stars bursting. They spill joy and hope across the fields, and I am so thankful to hear music again.

'We must not let go,' I tell you, as we walk back into the light.

Sunset from Dechomet Mountain

❧ April ❧

It's early April and our world is painted gold in the warmth of spring sunshine.

These mornings, I wake just before dawn. I am frightened in the wolf hour when my peace of mind is stolen and dark thoughts flood my mind like poison. The nightly news reports from local hospitals where people with the virus are struggling to breathe are terrifying.

'We could be dead within a month,' I think out loud, while the little birds in the hedgerows carry on singing in preparation for their big dawn chorus.

The early sun is intense and irresistible; it calls us to find peace on the pads and laneways. And so we walk often, watching the Spring lambs sporting and greeting neighbours along the way.

I want to explore old haunts and I'm taking you to the Master's Field, which lies at the bottom of a long, thin lane that leads to wild meadows. There's a circle of ancient oaks hidden in the bottom corner of the field. The trees are thin and gnarly with roots above ground, like arms outstretched, and they surround the thick stone walls of a former cabin dwelling that housed a hedge school in the 1800s. It's now tin-roofed, to provide shelter for cattle wintering out, but once upon a time it was a hidden seat of learning in a rocky barn, with a travelling teacher bringing fine verses of Latin and Irish along with the three Rs – home schooling in a wooded corner where primroses and ferns now spring from the stones.

We stand for a while thinking in the silence and then walk back up the lane. In the distance, we hear our neighbours' locked-down children learning and laughing in their gardens in the sunshine. Thankfully, they are all still growing in this storm.

I love these lemon dawns of April with the hedgerows full of sparrows and wrens, noisily nest building and praise giving. There is such comfort in the morning songs of blackbirds and thrushes, and I see their yellow notes fall softly from the trees, like flakes of sunshine. On the warmed grass, they melt into the score of the Earth's great song. The morning air is still and heavy with the scent of gorse blossoms that weave a saffron fringe around fields of waving, varnished grass.

'Gorse was the golden, spring star of the ancient Celts,' I tell you, as I light my daily candle of hope to put it in the window for those who have lost it. It's part of my routine now in this new reality and I want to remember it by keeping these notes about the transition happening in all our lives. The music performances we'd planned have been cancelled for the rest of the year but on the roof of the barn a pair of starlings are whistling and gurgling every morning.

On an evening walk late in the month, we stop to admire a herd of curious Hereford yearlings. Their dark red coats are glowing in the late sun as they come close to the gate, shaking their creamy heads and snorting playfully. The air is musky with the sweet scent of youth and gorse. I step closer to the gate and their leader takes off, cantering across the pasture. The others throw up their heads and follow – a glorious stampede of life racing into the horizon. It is impossible not to rejoice in their carefree energy and yet, deep down, I feel sorry for them because I know, in a few months' time, they will be taken from this field in a metal trailer to be sold. Their hooves will thunder against the steel prison as the vehicle drives away leaving an empty silence in the field. As a child growing up on a farm, this scene always saddened me. I am a vegetarian as a result.

When we get back to the house, I look up to the slopes and see a solitary sheep weaving her way through the stones and heather on to the grassy pad. 'It's Yoelene,' I tell you, walking quickly towards the hedge between our garden and the mountain. We watch her stepping daintily through the gravel until she stops at the bend on the path and returns my gaze with her wise, yellow eyes. Then she looks back to call her new-born lamb, stumbling bravely down the pad to keep close to its mother. She lifts her fine, horned head and looks across the valley to the Mourne kingdom. Mother and son are silhouetted against the deep, evening sky and my heart is bursting at the sight of Yoelene's prince. A tiny saviour.

The low sun is intense and floating in a faint rainbow circle that shimmers behind the mountain. It filters through the twilight clouds, hypnotic, astonishing.

The deepening light spreads and stains the horizon in pink and raspberry. This sunset is seeping across the evening sky and the Mourne kingdom is glowing in a rose-gold haze that settles in the East.

It's enchanting – East and West, setting and rising again. Dusk and dawn balancing the night sky, rocking the cradle of the Earth. Venus is hanging high and holding on to her place in the galaxy. She lights our path as we walk forward into May.

May Evening light

May

May is the month of wild, white flowers and limelight filtering through the morning foliage. The green Mayshine is dazzling as we float between the hedgerows – corridors bursting with cow parsley, chamomile and buttercups. The hedgerow chorus is glorious, with blackbirds, wrens and larks peeping and piping as their young dart in and out of the morning sun like staccato notes on a stave. Overhead, high above the mountain, the kites hang motionless in the warm breeze. They are elegant scavengers dropping with deadly precision to feed on young rabbits and roadkill. The daily business of the birds has become woven into our lives now. In the postbox on a pillar beneath the music barn, a scruffy, boisterous starling has set up home. The morning I found some leaves and strands of wool in the bottom of the box I knew it was no longer was ours – it had a higher purpose now. I looked up and saw her hopping and warbling on the rooftop. 'I'm glad you're back,' I whispered. Later, I put a plastic box on the ground at the gate and asked our postman to use it until the nursery was no longer required. Every day now, from the dark mouth of the postbox, we can hear the hungry cheeps of her babies shouting for food and company. When we've walked away, she'll deliver worms and insects and then patrol the driveway, warning off our cat Morphy and any other visitors. But sometimes she sits on the pillar just long enough to let us see her striking purple plumage flashing in the morning sun. She tilts her yellow-beaked head and I know she's thinking

'Can you see my dazzling, luminous feathers? Do you know who I am? Do you remember me?'

'I like her style – you'd think she owned the place,' you say, as we walk on.

'But she does,' I reply. 'I'm going to call her Blanche – she's dainty but a wee bit shabby.'

On the 5th of May we break new ground in a meadow that hasn't been cultivated in over a century. The meadow is a place apart on the farm as it sits within three crumbling stone walls at the top of a larger field facing the road. At one time it may have been a part of the mountain land, before the road was cut through at the base of the slopes, leaving this little triangular-shaped corner to find an identity of its own.

We are clearing the ground in the meadow to plant potatoes and wildflowers. The small, rusty gate is caught in the long, wild grass and we have to push it through into the brambled jungle of briars and gorse. Beneath the whins, we find scattered fieldstones, clay fire bricks and a rusted piece of a black, iron pot. They are the remnants of lives sheltered and warmed here in a rough cabin with an earthen floor over a century ago.

'A singer lived here once,' I tell you, looking at the clay bricks from a forgotten hearth. The meadow reminds me of this story my grandmother told about a woman called Maggie who lived here for a while. She was very poor and helped out on the local farms to get food. In summer, she walked the roads and the lanes singing and when she died, all the neighbours cried hard because she took all the songs with her.

I say a little prayer for Maggie as we start to lift the stones and set them back carefully among the gorse and ferns in the ditches. They are our witnesses to a new beginning for this old haven. When my cousin Paul arrives with his small digger to turn over the ground, the century-old sods break open smoothly like warm chocolate to breathe in the mountain air and start again.

In the big barn, the Mayshine is streaming through the clear, acrylic panels in the roof warming old wood and motes that are floating in the new light. High up on the gable wall there's a date scrawled in coarse lettering by my grandfather's hand – 'BD 1930'. The wall is built with uneven rocks and the mortar has loosened with time but it is still standing. Like many farmers of his generation, he left his mark on the stone. We dust off his iron horse ploughs and carry them slowly and carefully, feeling the weight of their years, out into the garden. I plan to paint them and let them shine again in the sun as new growth comes back on the farm.

By mid-May, the roadside banks are bowers of warm hawthorn toasting in the sunshine and the exotic, almond fragrance is sweet and comforting. These are the days our friendly, neighbouring cows dream of and the fields are full of sleepy Friesians who seem drugged as they stretch out flat in the warm grass. Overhead, the crows are loud and busy flying back and forward to their nest villages in the trees. A local farmer warns them to stay away from his newly sown crops by hanging a dead crow upside down on a gate. It stays there for months swaying in the wind.

The tree-top choirs of robins and wrens, black caps and blackbirds seem to call to us over and over again these mornings and their songs are irresistible. We continue to walk early but we are in no hurry. The tempo of our lives has been reset so we stroll between the hedgerows where everything is intertwined – briars, cow parsley, ferns, celandine, all making space for each other. In pockets beneath the brambles, bluebells add their simple, humble magic to the roadsides. Deep in the greenery, I believe the sprites are at large, singing as they gather fairy lace to make bridal gowns for the queens of May. And in the endless sunshine of these fragrant mornings, it is easy to forget the Covid storm.

'Was it ever here at all?' a neighbouring farmer asks.

'But of course it was here – so many have lost their lives,' I say.

'Sure they might have died anyway,' he says, lifting his buckets to walk on and feed his sheep.

You shake your head. 'He's afraid of the truth and he's not the only one.'

On the last evening of the month, we take the path up Dechomet Mountain to watch the sun set. Above us, a half-moon sits on a cloud curl watching the evening unfold, and in the distance, the Mournes shimmer in a rose-gold mirage. Up here, the distant townlands of Derryneil and Ballymagreehan are fringed with fire as the gorse glows in the deepening light. As we turn to face the west, Yoelene steps out of the gilded rushes and fixes us with her yellow-eyed stare.

'I like that she watches over us,' you say.

'I think she's been watching the world up here for a long time,' I reply. She looks away across the evening hills then wanders off to graze.

We watch the sun dissolve on the edge of our horizon and I close my eyes to listen. Across the townlands, in quiet ditches and meadows, there are bluebells ringing to give thanks for the Mayshine as we move on into June.

High on the Mountain

June

There's something about the smell of new rain that transforms a landscape. On the second of June, it falls softly in the night for the first time in two months. It lands silently on the mountain and, as the sun rises, the ground exudes a green sweetness and we welcome 'Gertrude', our first rose of summer, spreading her fragrant folds of pink velvet on the garden wall. We are on the road early in the fresh light, weaving in and out of the ground mists that float above the fields. The atmosphere is otherworldly and suddenly I see a bronze flash in the tall grass. We pause and wait in the misty silence. Then, for just a fleeting moment, a startled cock pheasant steps out of the haze to stare at us. He is splendid in his scalloped bronze and golden feathers that fold into a regal tail. Without thinking, I fold my hands and bow to him in thanks. He lifts his emerald head and disappears quickly into the swaying grasses.

'What a gift first thing in the morning,' I remark.

'It's always worth waiting at this time of day,' you say, as we follow the curve of the road into the waking valley.

Up on the hill fields, our donkeys are wading through buttercups and fragrant meadow grass. They have grown fat and sleepy in these humid, hazy days and sometimes I catch them dozing standing up with their tails flicking the summer flies. Neilly was a present from an old friend 20 years ago. He is small and sturdy with a thick, brown coat. His partner Sasha was a rescue donkey, homeless after her owner passed away. Together they've had a foal called Star and they live happily together on the hill idly watching the busyness of flies and people passing by. Our farrier arrives to trim their hooves and in his gentle voice he persuades them to lift their feet to be clipped and filed. We have been worried that he might not be allowed to visit given the Covid restrictions, but he tells me animal welfare is an 'essential service' and it's reassuring to know that, in this uncertain world, the animals have not been forgotten. The donkeys wander back into the field where Neilly and Sasha finish the grooming ceremony by nibbling and scratching each other's necks and shoulders.

For days, the valley bakes in a desert-like heat, and the shaven hay fields are crispy underfoot. Our neighbour says the rain that fell earlier this month was not the right kind of rain. 'It's not wetting the ground. The wind is carrying it away,' he says. Our world is heating up and we sense the birds know something is wrong. On the big electric cable hung across the mountain slopes, a cluster of starlings gather in a frenzy of clicks and chatter, twitching and nodding at every activity within their eyeline. On the Mountain Road, I am startled by a handful of screeching crows expelled upwards from the yawning blackness of a broken farmhouse. They are unsettled and land nervously on the dead branches of the lightning tree. I shiver and walk on, knowing something has happened somewhere today. On the evening news, there are reports of a huge dust cloud from the Sahara Desert blowing across the Caribbean and in the Arctic Circle the highest temperature ever has been recorded. It is 100 degrees in Siberia and the permafrost is melting.

In our meadow, the grass seed we sowed is pushing up from the old soil, searching for light, and in the scattering of stones around the base of the whins, I've planted alpine flowers and heathers. Sometimes I sit here around midday when the big, deep bell at Saint Mary of the Angels chapel resonates across the valley. I check the raised beds where the pink potato seeds are starting to flower and I hope that Maggie and the ancestors are nodding their approval somewhere, out there, high up above the Mournes.

Our world is bright with renewal for a while this month. As the lockdown restrictions are relaxed, we welcome family members back to the farm. It is good to share our stories and little triumphs in the meadow with those who care. The warmth of kinship and good neighbourliness is all around us and it is humbling. A five-year-old friend and his mother leave a home-baked wheaten loaf wrapped in foil over our fence, and we find fresh lettuce in a bag from another neighbour hung on the meadow gate.

On a clear June evening, I stop walking to admire the huge, broad leaves on an oak tree. They are strung on vivid crimson stems and are big enough to wrap a human heart in their emerald folds. In these happier days, I feel we are bundled up in an unexpected and kindly love.

Blanche continues to hop and scold from the sycamore as I pick up letters from the plastic box each morning. I can hear the chicks calling her from the black lip of the postbox. They are getting restless now.

'They'll be leaving soon,' you say. 'She'll lead them out early some morning when no one's around.'

The skies are silent and clear these days. There are no aeroplanes to stain the perfect blue so the heavens belong to the birds alone.

☙

On the 11th morning, Blanche is shouting on the roof of the music barn at five o'clock. I peep out through an upstairs window to watch her encouraging the young birds to step out into the world and spread their wings.

The exodus has begun, and by mid-morning the gaping mouth of the postbox is silent. 'You'll be glad to get rid of them,' says a neighbour, pointing at the white splashes of bird dirt beneath the box. But it's only dirt and it will wash away and already I miss the boisterous drama of Blanche and her brood. I look up into the treetops to find them but they are not there. Later, we open the door of the black box to reveal the huge nest that was their home. Layer upon layer of grass, ivy, wool and love. A tower of straw and song built to last, right up to the lip of the postbox, so the chicks had a secure base for their lift-off.

We are inspired by the beauty and strength of the nest. It is not just a home but a launch pad for the fledglings. In the evening, we are in a reflective mood and make plans to help some of your music students who have become disillusioned in the lockdown. Unable to perform, they cannot reach their potential. With gentle coaxing, we hope to help them prepare to step out and sing again .

On midsummer's eve, the June hedgerows are heavy with greenery. Ferns, eucalyptus, foxgloves and elderflowers are spilling on to the verges. The huge elderflower heads balance like saucers of champagne on their elegant stems, offering us countless reasons to celebrate the freedom of summer evenings.

In the meadow, we gather rough and ancient stones from the ditches to trace a circle on the soft rise of the lea. It will be a bed for wildflower and music seedlings to grow together.

On the last day of June it has been 100 days since this lockdown began. On the edge of dark, a huge creamy moon slides up over the hill from Slievenaboley. She is bright and intense, slipping in and out of the cloud islands like another Earth floating in the sapphire sky. The world keeps turning and we are full of hope so we keep moving on with our plans, following the light into July.

View from the Windy Gap

July

Early July and we are walking in a rippling sea of green. All around the mountain, the second silage crops are strong and growing urgently while our neighbour, whom I call the Captain, sits on his high yellow harvester, waiting patiently with his wagons on the field boundaries. Every day now, we hear the familiar rumble of the mowers echoing around the valley from early morning until dusk. The harvesting has a compulsion and an importance all of its own and the Captain knows this as he keeps one eye on the clock and another on the sky.

The countryside is busy with harvest traffic, so we walk off the road on the quiet pads and lanes that criss-cross the hills. There is a race for freedom in the hedgerows as plants seem to scramble for their place in the green banks. Year after year, dockens, briars, eucalyptus and ferns find a way to share the space in the ditches and they lean out eagerly to greet us.

'And look,' I say to you, 'here they come – the dandies of the ditch!'

We laugh because there's something about dandelions that makes us happy. They are like little yellow rosettes of sunshine pinned into the verges. A prize for keeping going, perhaps, in these difficult times. The Covid threat still lurks unseen and stealthy in the undergrowth of our lives but the restrictions are easing and on the 4th of July you return to the city to play music at regular gigs in a hotel that has been closed since March. We cannot yet host performances for an audience in the barn but we can record individual players for short concerts online. It's not what we imagined but it is good to make plans to bring music back to the farm.

In these slow, humid days we feel we are living in a borrowed reality that is half the life it once was. For our animal companions, life goes on without analysis and they provide many dramas, joys and sorrows. Captain Tom is a ginger cat in the wild tribe of feral cats you feed at a neighbouring farm every morning. He is a gentleman, polite and kind, circling the team to make sure all the others get fed before he eats. On a heart-breaking morning, you find him weak and distressed. We lift him gently into the cat box and I drive carefully out of the yard, leaving the rest of the tribe sitting in a circle watching him go. A few hours later, the vet calls to say he has been poisoned and has passed away. Our hearts are empty and sad and all I can say to you is that he knew he was loved in that circle of friends and his gentle spirit will rest forever in these hills.

In the meadow, our potato plants are growing tall and strong and wise neighbours advise that it's time to spray them to protect from blight.

'It's probably 150 years since potatoes were last grown here,' I tell you, and I can't help but wonder about the people who lived here back in the 1800s, and if they survived the Famine. Sometimes, when the light is clear, we can see ridged tracks of the lazy beds hastily created on Slieve Croob to move the potato crop to higher ground. From the meadow, we can also see them way out on the blue distant Mournes – fear and desperation traceable on the mountainscape to this day. I lift the broken piece from the black iron potato pot and set it back among the old stones in the ditch. Another remnant of the past, it knows the story as it watches and waits while we carry on spraying and praying that our strong plants don't turn black, curl up and rot.

These long evenings, we walk until late, watching the landscape rebuild itself like a giant jigsaw. The lights on the fleet of blue silage wagons form a luminous parade as they roll back and forward loading fodder for the winter days ahead. The waving fields of green become pale, shorn pastures where the crows drop like stones to pick for seeds and insects.

On the mountain, freshly sheared sheep look fat and comfortable in their birthday suits as they chew thoughtfully. Yoelene takes her evening strolls with her plump lamb high up near the cairn. She can see so much from this viewing point. The Mourne peaks to the south-east, Lough Neagh and the Sperrins to the north-west and the long, silent Belfast Hills beyond Slieve Croob. I wonder did her old soul see the people build their lazy beds in vain. I wonder if she saw

Maggie on the road singing a lament for what was lost back then. Sometimes she just stares out into the west, transfixed, as we often are, by the setting sun that lingers and then flatlines on the curve of our amber horizon.

On the last day of July, we welcome Ciaran, an old friend who is a musician lost without his audience. It is so uplifiting to hear him play his saxophone with you in the music barn, which has been dark for too long. Charlie Parker classics played at break-neck speeds spill out across the farmyard and into the fields, creating a radiant sheet of sound. Afterwards, we celebrate with a feast of cabbage and the first potatoes from the meadow. Something godly has happened and the music has lifted our souls. There is lively talk about John Coltrane and Paddy Kavanagh, blue trains and mystical mountains. Meanwhile, beyond our hills and high up above the Mournes, a small, marmalade cat curls up in the arm of a pale, crescent moon waiting patiently for the first August morning.

Touching the Sky on Slieve Croob

✤ August ✤

It's the first Sunday in August and we are in the meadow early with the potatoes and herbs. The smell of chocolate mint mingled with parsley and rosemary is heady and luxurious. The herb cuttings were gifts from kind neighbours and this little acre feels enriched with kindness. Good deeds are growing in the rich, old soil and in the high, wild hedge honeysuckle clusters dance and nod at the tiny raspberries peeping out below. I love that this little piece of rescued ground has opened its old heart to us and is giving so freely. I hope that somewhere out there, above the clouds, Maggie is watching and singing.

In the late morning, we have gathered with friends at the foot of Slieve Croob to do the annual Blaeberry Sunday walk. It's named after the wild blue bilberries (known as blaeberries locally) but some also call it Cairn Sunday as, for centuries, people have walked to the summit, bringing a stone to place on the 12 cairns marking the burial grounds of ancient kings. The tradition also celebrates the old harvest festival Lughnasa in honour of the Celtic god Lugh – bringer of sun and light. My mother grew up here with her brothers and sisters in the parish of Finnis. I'm thinking of her today as the summit slips in and out of misty cloud wisps. As the midday sun starts to burn them off, we can see more clearly the distant Sperrins, the Mournes, Belfast and Strangford lough.

'I have that feeling again that the world is at my feet,' I tell you.

'Well, we're almost touching the clouds,' you answer, staring back at the path that seems to disappear off the mountain and into the sky.

The line is thin up here – a march ditch I sense between Heaven and Earth.

The mountain is warm, damp and fragrant with sponges of purple heather and bog cotton softening our path across the slopes. We descend briskly on the boggy ground, passing the stiles and hidden streams that feed into the Lagan, which emerges in the peaceful fields of Dree below us. We arrive at the Pass Loanin and I sense a step back in time, walking the path my mother and her sisters often took. Their laughter is sweet on the breeze, filtering through the old trees, and it is good to continue the tradition of this journey with them.

These evenings, we sometimes sit in the meadow watching the light changing on the face of the Mournes. Out on the road, the fleet of blue trailers is still bringing home the harvest, sailing like cargo boats between the hedgerows. The ebb and flow of the trailer parade is dignified and time-honoured, marking Lughnasa like their ancestors before them. Their flashing lights circle the mountain until the harvest is gathered and their Captain, cruising high above the hedge-line, steers his tall, yellow galleon homewards.

Mid-August brings grey skies and heavy hearts. The R number is straining and the virus is spreading again. Some blame youthful excesses – a generation partying because for so long it's felt like there's no tomorrow.

'The young ones let us down,' a neighbour says

'It's not fair to blame them,' I cry.

We are continuing with our plan to open the music barn for young performers to rehearse in safely. Our young friends Mickey and Oisín return to the farm with their guitars and banjos to write and rehearse their music. The barn lamp glows as they strike their bright notes and share their new songs and, for a while, we are all feeling lifted and resilient.

The peace does not last long, though, as the skies are darkening, and on the 19th, Storm Ellen brings the full force of her hurricane-strength winds to the mountains. In the garden, there's a trail of broken dahlias, lupins and cosmos and our wildflower babies are shivering like snowdrops. The mountain soaks in dark green tones as the summer grass is swamped by endless rain and cattle struggle to drag their heavy bodies through the sucking, squelching earth. The health minister warns of another lockdown and we take to the roads to walk through the worry.

These days, the Mournes are hidden behind a grey veil for days. It is unsettling to watch the empty sky in the distance.

'I am lost without them,' I tell you. 'I cannot hear their choirs.'

We need a change of scene, and on a dry, breezy afternoon we walk round the lake in Castlewellan Forest Park. There's a low, green mist floating just above the forest floor after the days of rain. The air is damp and thick with the scent of cedars and pines — it is refreshing and almost intoxicating. Under the dark forest canopy the atmosphere is peculiar and otherworldly. Throaty wood pigeons gurgle to each other across the high, thin pines that lean over the emerald lake, staring at their reflected grandeur. We walk in silence, thinking many things about what the future holds.

A few days later, Storm Francis blows in from the Atlantic at four o'clock in the morning and the wolf is back at his work, stealing our sleep and peace of mind. This summer is broken — lying in pieces like the branches strewn across the fields. Our huge sycamore is waving like a feather in the winds that send bulbous clouds rolling out across Slieve Croob. In the meadow, we stake the dahlias, lupins and sweet peas once again. From the road, you point up to the fairy thorn still bound stubbornly to the mountain slope. In my mind's eye, I can see the huge roots dug in like a claw on the stony ditch. Beneath the whins, Yoelene stands resolutely with her back to the east wind, and the rest of her tribe stand in quiet dignity with her. They just keep going.

In the morning, the unexpected sunshine is so welcome and it is good to be dazzled again. In the farmyard, we feed chopped carrots to the donkeys and watch a parade of swallows line up like ballerinas on the barn roof. They step lightly as they shift from side to side, chattering and lifting to pirouette in the warm air. It is a blessing to watch their graceful dance. On the last evening of this month we walk down over the Rock and up the Common Hill. The crows are roosting in the old fir trees below the Mine Corner, noisily picking their branches and jawing with one another. The hedgerows are glossy now with wet ivy and the first hawthorn berries warm the ditches.

The dying embers of our last August sun are sinking in the west and the swallows have all lifted in a feathered haze. In a breath they are gone. Their summer dance is over. September rises tomorrow.

Two roads diverge in Castlewellan Forest Park

September

September dawn breaks like crystal, casting a blonde, mystical light across the Mournes. The fields below are steeped in three days' rain and make a thick, sucking sound underfoot, but up on the slopes white water flashes triumphantly as it cascades over polished granite. We are walking early on the Rathfriland road, which starts to rise five miles away out of the village of Dromara. As it weaves its way up and over the braes, the air gets cooler and the mists get lower. At the soft curve where the road starts to sweep back down into the valley, we stop to take in the view from the Boiling Well, where a mountain stream emerges from the hills in a bubbling frenzy. It is caught in a small, square tank on the roadside, rewarding visitors with endlessly fizzing water that dances in the light before disappearing into the river in the belowland. For centuries, people have drunk from the well believing that the water provides healing and good health; a cup still hangs above the babbling pipe to this day. From somewhere deep down in these ancient hills, the spring has determinedly found its way upwards through rock strata and soil to burst out into the light. Mountain water flowering on the hillside – pure and timeless.

Our quiet roads and loanins are heavy with riches in September. A soft wind breathes in and out through the sycamores like an autumn tide washing away the footprints of summer. In its wake, the hedgerows are awash with bursts of scarlet hawthorn berries and orange sloes. Their fruit striking the big, red notes of the season is so warming and welcome and, for a while, there is a peace in knowing the Earth's great song is changing key for a deeper, slower melody.

In the music barn, our friend Scott arrives to play the piano for a recording to be shared online with audiences who miss the experience of live performances. Hearing Gershwin in the lamplight is emotional and the melancholy notes of 'Someone to Watch Over Me' seem to linger in the still evening air. You lift your trumpet to accompany him on 'I'll Be

Seeing You'. The piece is sad but comforting and could not be more appropriate in these anxious times when everyone is missing their friends and the Covid storm is still brewing.

Mid-September brings a bitter wind and the Mountain Road is crisp underfoot with parched leaves that fall silently like golden feathers. We walk briskly onwards through the amber evening lights that are ever changing on the Mourne peaks. On the Common Hill, wood smoke is wreathing above a scalded hedgerow, and the smell of spitting, burning hawthorn is bittersweet. Above, a hooded crow tears purposefully across the twilight and returns with six more comrades. They settle, loudly scawing and scolding on a telephone wire. 'What news is breaking here?' I wonder. We walk back quickly to the farmyard, thankful to see the warm lights at the gate. As we cross the yard, you raise your hand to stop at the doorway and bend down to examine a small, black body on the tarmac. It's a bat – a pipistrelle with a masked fox face, blindly crawling in the shadows. I have never seen a bat on the farm before and am unsure what to do with our lost visitor. We decide to leave it for a while in the hope it will fly home but, in the morning, we find it still crawling near the hallway. On the advice of the local bat group, we lift the tiny pipistrelle and put him in a soft box with water in a bottle top. We leave him with a prayer for another night.

On the evening news, David Attenborough is warning the world to wake up and protect our planet. He says the world's wildlife is under the greatest ever threat with humans clearing forests on a massive scale for farming. The destruction of natural habitats is causing the disturbance and death of so many creatures and two lonely white rhinos in Kenya, the last of their species, are the symbols of what we have lost. We sit in silence thousands of miles away listening to David's warning. Everything seems out of time on our planet with the natural rhythms disturbed.

The next morning, we are saddened to find our pipistrelle has not survived. A little displaced soul blown off course on life's journey. I wonder where his home was and why he lost his way. We lay him to rest in a small, wooden box until our bat group friend calls to take him away.

As the autumn equinox approaches, the sun is rising later and the night falls earlier. 'We need to start gathering light to get us through the winter,' I tell you, half-jokingly, on a bright day when we are walking in Castlewellan Forest Park. 'We'll need all we can get,' you reply. The latest news is depressing; the number of Covid-related deaths is rising again. Our government has announced new restrictions including a complete ban on live music performance. It feels like the lights have been switched off again. We walk on silently through the autumn scenes in the forest, foraging for hope. From somewhere deep amongst the trees, a lone blackbird strikes her note and holds on to it, endlessly repeating her soulful melody.

The air is musky and pine-smoked under the canopy of cedars and cypresses. We are walking on a pad that stretches forever into the secret woods and I breathe deeply, trying to absorb this silken light. September is falling, silently, all over the golden forest floor and the giant drooping juniper weeps for our lost summer.

Linley on the Moat pad walking towards Dechomet Mountain

October

On the first day of this mellow month, the sky above the Mountain Road is a pristine blue, swept clean of all September's debris. The chocolate fields of Closkelt and Katesbridge are peaceful in the first frosted mists of the season. I'm standing in a short lane perfectly lined with six aged oak trees facing each other on either side as they guard the passageway now filled with crisp curls of fallen leaves.

'When did your stories begin?' I wonder. 'Did someone plant you here carefully a few centuries ago or did you self-seed to grow as companions for each other in this quiet field?'

The lane opens into a small, abandoned farmyard and the ruins of the old farmhouse walls support an ugly hole in the collapsed roof. Like many abandoned dwellings in these hills, the house looks shocked by the ravages of time. It must have been a cosy home for a family once with its neat, oak-lined lane and a view across the valley. I close my eyes and picture a hearth with turf piled up and a flat griddle with soda bread rising and a tilly lamp casting a golden glow around the room.

I can picture Maggie walking these roads looking for fallen branches and briars to make a fire in her cottage in the meadow. I see her standing on this lane wishing she owned this little house with its hearth and stool and all. As I turn to face the sun and move on from the melancholy scene, a handful of scolding crows lift from the dark hole and chase me along the road. It's their home now – a safe place to roost in the encroaching winter.

October is the month the clocks change and we must prepare to reset for the shorter days. We are walking lots on the brightest mornings, collecting light for our hearts' winter store. A little song keeps repeating in my head and I've no idea where it came from. Maybe it's a chorus from a previous life that wants to be remembered. Maybe Maggie sang it as she collected firewood on the mountain.

'I'll go gathering light for you and bring it home in armfuls,

And when the winter shadows fall, we'll have lanterns by the barnful…'

The unfinished song makes me smile as I set off humming into the autumn hills.

On a dazzling Sunday mid-month, we make our way to the Lighthouse Road near Leitrim village. From the small carpark with a spectacular view of the Mournes, the signs for the Moat Pad Footpath take us off road and on to a grassy lane. The wooden gate clicks behind us and immediately I sense we're in another place in time. A century ago, this ancient path was used by children walking, often barefoot, to the National School in Dechomet. The hedgerows on either side are high and heavy with gorse and hawthorn. It's like a secret passageway that beckons you to come forward. This is fox land – musky ditches punched with secret dens that reach deep into the hillside. At night, these hills belong to them and we often hear their screaming barks echo across the valley.

The pad is springy underfoot and rises over the drumlin to give way to granite stone-walled fences that lead to open farmland. The moat that gave the path its name is long gone but the Norsemen must have known the best route over these hills. As we make our way down Adder's Loanin, the 12 peaks of the Mournes emerge to our left, shimmering in the bright, cold air; before us, Dechomet Mountain rises in all its glory. The summit is soft and rounded with an impressive display of granite standing stones and circles.

'The Vikings named it well,' I tell you. 'Dechomet means 'good viewing or look out post'.'

It is exhilarating to walk in this dappled, golden light with cheerful wrens chit-chatting in the thinning gorse hedgerows. The red kites love these days of warm currents and coast gracefully in their bubbles high above the mountain. With their flashing red breasts, they are like bronzed messengers of hope floating above an October lane where time has stopped and the worried world has paused to step back and reflect.

'Look how far we've come,' you say, staring back at the meandering pad, which disappears over the brow of the hill.

As the days grow shorter, we miss music performance more and more. The government's Covid restrictions still ban all live shows. Although we and our families have managed to stay safe so far in this pandemic, infection rates are spiralling throughout the country. And so our barn, a place of warmth and shelter for music to grow in, is empty and silent. It feels like Covid has killed the flame and the world is getting darker every day.

'We will find another way,' you say. 'Music always finds a way.'

The twilight skies in October are atmospheric and enchanting as the pale, setting sun casts a yellow glow behind the mountain. The starlings love this light and we sometimes stand in a daze at the crossroads watching a murmuration whirling across the horizon.

'There goes Blanche with her tribe,' you say, and we smile at the thought of our bird with her chicks flying freely in the supportive mass of her clan.

On the day the clocks change, I go back to the forest in Castlewellan to see the last of the autumn light. Following the path around the lake is calming and restorative. The giant sequoias and maples are strong and silent, breathing in and out as they have done for centuries. They are sure of their place in the forest, co-existing with the firs and cypresses. From deep in the woods a bellowing bull stalks in the undergrowth like a lost soul looking for home. The geese on the lake hear him and rise in a riot of trumpeting calls. The woods are suddenly alive with sound energy and the afternoon light deepens in green and gold between the trees. I breathe in and walk on.

On the 31st October, the prime minister announces another lockdown, and on the coastline Storm Aiden tears into the country with 30-foot-high tidal waves. On this All Hallows Eve, the wind is screaming in the telephone wires strewn across the mountain. The veil is thin between our world of the living and that of the dead. We are lying low beneath the whins once again and holding on to remembered light.

Mournes as the cloud lifts

November opens with a sombre sky that is cloud-heavy and bruised after the storms. We walk into a broken landscape on Drumgooland Road. Snapped branches litter the verges beneath the tired trees and swollen streams bleed out into the empty fields. The road is flooded in places with pothole pools – cloud puddles mirroring the grey and empty sky. Our steps are faltering and we feel out of time once again.

In the distance, a wide cap cloud sits above the Mournes, so the peaks are hidden. I am unsettled when I can't see the mountains. The familiar blue curves of the range are powerful and reassuring. We walk on in an uneasy silence, and I'm longing for a singing bird to fill the distant void.

In my head I start to recite the names of their 12 peaks to pray them back, counting off the names on my fingers:

Slieve Donard named after the holy man Domangard

Commedagh the mountain of watching

Binian the mountain of the little horns

Bearnagh the broken mountain with a gap between its twin summits

Lamagan the mountain to be crawled up using hands and feet

Meelbeg the mountain of the small animals

Meelmore the mountain of the large animals

Slieve Muck the mountain of the pig

Slievenaglogh the two mountains of the stones, and

Ben Crom the mountain of the curved peak

The names are rich, full of stories and music. Every one of these grand summits has earned its place in the 12. Born out of fire and ice, they shine in this granite parade and the repetition of their names is as soothing as a prayer.

I think the naming of a mountain is so important – an acknowledgement of its power and unique character. I feel sorry for the lonely little hills that don't have names but are also so important in the contours of this horizon. All the fields on our farm have names and I drew a rough map of them years ago so I wouldn't forget: Rose's Park, Kearney's Hill, The Point and The Wee Field. The land holds memories forever and they are the foundations of the special kind of love that exists between a person and a place.

As we turn the corner at the end of the Mountain Road, a gleam of sunlight – a glisk – seeps out behind the solid cloud gradually spreading new light over the 12. The sun has found them and wants them to shine once again. Someday, when this storm passes, we will go there to walk in the Kingdom of Mourne, but for now it is enough that they form the boundary of our imaginations. We move on healed and enlightened by the moment.

On the way home we pass the field where the Herefords sported. It's empty now. Most of the cattle that haven't been sold have been taken into slatted sheds for winter storage. The countryside is quiet and cold so, late in the month, we go back to the woods in Castlewellan to be with the trees and the lake. We come to a fork on the forest road. To the left, the way is bright and clear, lined with young elm trees. To the right, a saffron alleyway heavy with shedding maples disappears into the yellow woods.

'Let's stay on this road,' you say.

And so we walk on into the yellow woods and make plans to plant another crowd of daffodils in the fairy circle.

The days are shorter now and the hedgerows are thin and bare but on bright days they are full of chattering wrens and finches looking for winter shelter. Their little songs light up the tired ditches but it is our garden robin who sings the highest notes. Every morning now, Paddy is hopping on the fence. It is impossible to miss the scarlet flash on the hedge as he watches me carry the nuts and seeds out to our bird table. Sometimes, he rewards us when he lands to swing on a briar hoop hanging down from a hedge. His winter song is a welcome blessing from all our soul friends out beyond the horizon.

On the last evening of the month, I am walking on the Common Hill at the edge of dark. The mountain is quiet and soft as the pale sun slips down through the black lace of winter branches. I hear the soft rasp of a yard brush on a farmyard floor and the lowing of settling cows munching silage. The crows are hushed now on their roosts and in the flat field on the hilltop, two horses graze gently on the winter grass. A chestnut and a grey, they are statuesque and otherworldly as they lift their heads to sniff the evening air. Behind them, Slieve Croob waits in the distance for Saint Michael's evening church bells to ring. The mountain is so powerful and peaceful up there where the cairns touch the sky and I do believe it is to this sacred place that love goes when we lose someone dear. All the souls and the saints remembered this month are shimmering somewhere out there between Heaven and Earth. Slowly, out of the navy horizon, a huge apricot moon is rising higher and higher above the mountainscape. In the glowing, perfect silence of this moment, the chestnut, the grey and I watch this old month dissolve under the radiant light of a Full Beaver Moon.

Winter Sun on Drumgooland Road

December

It's the first of December and we have crossed over the starlit bridge to Winter.

Last night's moon burnt a pathway through the constellations above these hills and we can see the road ahead more clearly. It is the glistening road to Advent and the solstice – to the coming of the light. On this crisp Sunday morning we are following the rising sun on the Mountain Road. It fills the valley with strands of a rose-gold mist that is threaded through the waking townlands of Leitrim, Gargory and Clanmaghery. I am leaning on my grandfather's old farmyard gate, which we have cleaned down with a wire brush and painted red. It has been reborn and now hangs on a new granite pillar to create a welcoming entrance to the frosted meadow. On the top bar, little frozen beads of time are melting in the morning sun. I watch them slip away like the years on the gate. In a shining minute they are gone, dissolving into the meadow grass and the little river where they will begin their journey again.

We walk on between the wintering hedgerows where decaying ferns have found a soft landing on the damp grass. Together with the fallen leaves, they have been laid to rest and returned to the soil. Overhead, the oaks and sycamores lean in towards each other as if for warmth and their canopy throws a latticed sunlight across the road. For over a century, children from the back of the mountain walked this way to Dechomet Primary School. On golden mornings like this, I hear their laughter and their chatter mingling with the sound of their first steps on this road to learning. They are little pilgrims seeking the truths that can only be found on a country road. The sweet, yellow notes of a blackbird in early spring; The music of a mountain stream that spills out of a hedge like a waterfall in miniature; the enduring fragrance of the hedgerows filled with gorse and hawthorn, honeysuckle and dog roses. We walk on behind them enjoying the peace of this dusky morning.

In the days that follow, the sun is strong, and the news gets better. A vaccine has been approved for distribution starting this month. Hopes are pinned to the glorious superstar that will appear soon when Jupiter and Saturn align. The world feels brighter already with the prediction of the healing light. We have never needed to hear music more and in the pause before Christmas, we record some of our young friends performing in the barn. Niamh, a fledgling with soulful soprano tones, sings Christmas jazz with your trio.

'Here we are as in olden days, happy golden days of yore.
*Faithful friends who are dear to us will be near to us once more.'**

The warm, familiar melodies shine and are so welcome after the silence. The moment is a brief respite, though, as the corona storm is still raging on the fringes of our reality. Another lockdown is called for and fear lurks high up in the black winter trees where the crows have roosted. They are waiting in the frozen silence for the longest night of the year to end. I put a candle in the window and ask you to play something joyous. The bright notes of *Gloria in Excelsis Deo* fill our home with hope and your music spills out across the mountain, soaring upwards to the new Star of Bethlehem.

On the 21st solstice morning, Paddy robin waits for me in the glistening hawthorn. His flaming red, sacred little heart is a beacon on this deep midwinter day when the Earth pauses on its axis and waits for the sun to carry us over the frozen line. It's a landmark day and we are ready for a change. We take the high, rocky path up Dechomet Mountain to watch the sun rise like the first people did centuries before us. December is gifting us her best light before the sky drains at the end of the month, when the land will be purified and ready to start again. From the summit, a 360-degree view of our world is caught in a dazzling, yellow spell: The Sperrins, Lough Neagh, the Belfast Mountains, the lowlands around Strangford and, just across the valley, Slieve Croob and all our familiar hills. Finally, my gaze settles on the Mourne kingdom. The 12 peaks are sparkling in a haze of snow dust. On a slender hawthorn branch, Paddy robin sits amongst the beads of time praising the scene with his loveable song. The light is coming back and it is unstoppable.

---

* From the song 'have yourself a merry little Xmas' by R Blane/H Martin

We are standing on the summit, surrounded by cairns and folds of ancient stones. They are the silent witnesses to all the ceremonies that must have happened here before. The fires of celebration and of warning; the loving and the living that is buried deep beneath the heather and the moss here. On the cairn, the ancient people placed their stones to leave their mark as a memorial to their very existence. In some of the rocks, there are soft indents where rainwater has settled, creating little stone bowls of light – offerings to the sun god. Without thinking, I put my hand in the water and make the sign of the cross.

We are rooted in a plantation of stones, smoothed and tuned with the passing of the years. They are printed on the slopes like notes on a score sheet. It feels like we are in time with the mountains once again and our cheeks are burning as we lift our canes to follow the path back to home.

In the evening, we make plans to grow a community to support Niamh and other emerging singers. We invite friends who are songwriters, vocal coaches, producers and experienced musicians to form a musical flock with us to support young performers who have not learnt how to fly in this difficult year. We hope that together we will gain strength for the unknown journey that lies ahead next year. Outside, the two worlds of Jupiter and Saturn align to present the Christmas Star above the mountain. I have no doubt it is a blessing from beyond.

On the last day of the month, snow is falling silently like frozen, white feathers all over our world. The hills are quiet now and the old year's storms are just memories. I cannot hear the birds but I know Blanche and her flock are out there waiting for the spring trees to waken. Up on Dechomet Mountain, Yoelene stands alone amongst our footprints in the snow. From a distance, I see us all painted into this landscape forever now.

It is time to move on. Tomorrow will be the 1st of January 2021 and we will go back to Slieve Croob to begin again.

Footprints on the mountain

Epilogue

On the 1st of January 2021 there was an extraordinary, volcanic sunset over the Mourne kingdom. Slieve Donard seemed to breathe fire up into the sky and the kingdom glowed underneath the plumes of red-gold clouds. We watched the show from the meadow, once again in awe of the light on the mountains.

As the month progressed, we prepared the ground for a new project called the Magy's Farm Collective. It's a creative flock of music producers, mentors and coaches coming together to support the development of young artists online and using our barn as a rehearsal and performance space. To date, five singers have written and recorded 25 original songs. Niamh released her first EP in September 2021 and her debut show at the Cathedral Quarter Arts Festival in Belfast was a sell-out. Music seems to like growing here.

Blanche came back in May 2021 and built her nest once again in the postbox. I think she wants to live beside us here as an equal and she is so welcome. We continue to walk with the wild chorus, grateful to be in tune and in time with the seasons on the mountains.

✤ Acknowledgements ✤

My sincere thanks to these good people who inspired and encouraged me to write this book:

Professor Ian Sansom (School of Creative Arts, University of Warwick)

Dr Garrett Carr and Dr Sam Thompson from the School of Arts, English and Languages at the Seamus Heaney Centre, Queen's University Belfast.

Kerri ni Dochartaigh – nature writer and mentor (kerrinidochartaigh on Instagram)

Kathryn Aalto – author and educator (kathrynaalto.com)

Colin Harper – author, composer and owner of Belfast Proofreading

Mark Case at Whitenoise Studios

Nigel and Theresa at biddles.co.uk

Dr Linley Hamilton – my darling husband and guiding light (magysfarm.co.uk)

I would like to thank all these musicians and singers who have supported us and performed at Magy's Farm to date and we look forward to many more happy, inspirational evenings in the music barn.

Kyron Bourke, Jude Johnstone, Ray Duncan, Foy Vance, FSQ String quartet, Blue Orchard, Dana Masters and band, Paul Dunlea Quartet, John Donegan Quartet, Jim Beard and Jon Herington, Scott Flanigan, Ken Haddock, and the Ari Hoenig Trio with Conor Chaplin and Tom Ollendorff.

Grateful and heartfelt thanks to these producers and coaches in our Collective

Pete Doherty, Michael Mormecha, Matt Curran, Rocky O'Reilly, Dave Marks, Jude Johnstone, Dana Masters, Liane Carroll and Foy Vance.

And finally, I want to wish every success to all these young artists in our Magy's Farm Collective

Niamh Murray, Lara O Donnell, Cara Quinn, Rhian Brownlow, Clodagh Biggs and Dominique Mullin

May you all find your wings and fly into the light.

Neilly and Sasha

All proceeds from this book will be donated to thedonkeysanctuary.org.uk

❧ About the Author ❧

Maggie Doyle grew up on a hill farm in the townland of Dechomet in the Dromara Hills, County Down. She worked for BBC Northern Ireland as a radio producer and manager for over thirty years and, after taking early retirement in 2019, she returned to live on the farm with her husband Dr Linley Hamilton.

Linley is a musician, educator and broadcaster and together they run a music club and the Magy's Farm Collective which is a mentoring scheme to support young singer/songwriters and musicians.

'Mountain Notes' is based on the diary Maggie kept during 2020. It documents the early days of the music club before the Covid-19 pandemic brought restrictions on live performances across the world. Like so many people in lock down, Maggie and Linley went walking regularly in their local landscape.

This book is an affectionate and lyrical memoir of their re-connection with the natural world in the mountains all around them and the re-imagining of the farm as a place where music grows.

Maggie graduated from Queen's University Belfast with an MA in Creative Writing with Distinction in December 2021. This is her first book.

❧